YOU SLEPT *where* LAST NIGHT?

By
Tim Conway

PRICE STERN SLOAN, INC.
Los Angeles

Cover art and illustrations by Chuck Reasoner
Photographs by Roger Fuhr of ROLANDesign
Certain graphic symbols reprinted from Handbook of
Pictorial Symbols by Rudolf Modley, Dover Press

Copyright © 1985 by Tim Conway
Illustrations copyright © 1985 by Price Stern Sloan, Inc.
Published by Price Stern Sloan, Inc.
360 North La Cienega Boulevard, Los Angeles, California 90048

ISBN: 0-8431-1239-5

TABLE OF CONTENTS

DEDICATION

For helping give this book a place for itself among the indispensable reference books of its time, I thank Abbie, Adelle, Aggie, Alexa, Angela, Arlene, Babs, Bea, Belle, Betty-Lou, Blaze, Blossom, Bunni, Candi, Carli, Cici, Cheri, Christi, Cindi, Danielle, Darla, Dawn, Debbi, Dolly, Dyanne, Drucie, Edie, Effie, Ellen, Emmylou, Eunice, Fanny, Fleur, Flo, Gabrielle, Georgette, Gertie, Goldy, Gudrin, Hazel, Hedwig, Hildegarde, Honi, Indira, Inga, Ingrid, Inez, Jacqui, Janee, Jasmine, Jewel, Jo, Joyce, Jynx, Kandi, Kristi, Kyla, Lala, Letti, Lilac, Linda, Lisa, Lola, Mabel, Maddie, Mai, Marci, Marylin, Mavis, Mindi, Nanette, Natasha, Nellie, Nita, Nona, Olga, Ona, Ora, Pandora, Patience, Patsi, Prunella, Queene, Quinn, Randi, Raye, Rena, Robbyne, Romy, Roz, Rula, Sadi, Salome, Shari, Star, Sunnie, Taffy, Tammy, Trixie, Ursula, Velma, Velvet, Wanda, Wendy, Xaviera, Yolanda, Zazu, Zoe and Zora.

DON'T MINIMIZE
THE IMPORTANCE OF THIS BOOK

This may be the most important book you ever pick up.
It is a book that will be immensely valuable to many
people. Its lessons are not restricted to those who, in
the words of the author, inadvertantly "fool around."
It will be valuable to those who have ever been exposed
to the possibility of "fooling around." Or who used to
think about "fooling around." Or who think they might
someday "fool around." Or, most importantly, who know
someone else who "fools around."

Until now, you've had no option but to silently suffer
the indignity of the insinuating, "You slept *where* last
night?" Now you have an answer. Many foolproof
answers. All you have to do is turn the page and you'll
never again be the victim of such false and unfair accu-
sations. Now go ahead and start with the most important
advice of all: getting into the house undetected.

HOW TO SNEAK INTO THE HOUSE UNDETECTED

Once you have decided to actually enter the house, there are a few key things to keep in mind. First of all, remember you are entering a potential battleground. The enemy could be lurking in the most unsuspecting places. As my old sergeant used to say, "Keep your eyes open and your rear down." The following pages are devoted to a foolproof technique developed after many years. If followed to the letter, it will allow you to return safely and securely to the nest or conjugal bed.

1. THE APPROACH

As you approach your house, turn the ignition off and coast into the yard or garage.

If you have power brakes, construct a "car stopper" in your garage. This consists of several tires lined up on the rear wall.

2. MOTOR COOLER

The moment the car stops, cool the motor with a hose, just in case your partner wakes up and feels the hood to see if it's still hot.

It's not a bad idea to hose down the tires also. If you know of an all-night car wash, run your car through a couple of times before going home.

3. LOOK YOURSELF OVER

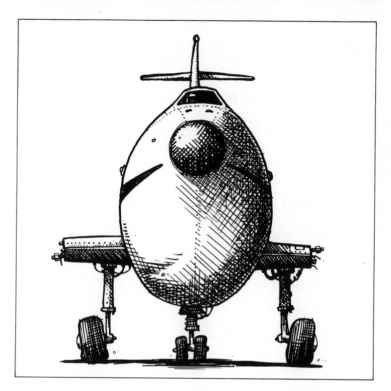

When arriving home late we sometimes worry so much about the excuse that we fail to take a good look at ourselves. Pilots call it the "walk around."
Before they get into their plane, they walk around it to make sure everything is intact. For instance, does the plane have wings; is there a runway near-by?...etc.

The following pages are devoted to the pre-entry check lists.

LOOK YOURSELF OVER...

CHECK LIST #1: AM I DRUNK?

If you have trouble answering eight or more of the following, wait five minutes before entering the house.

_____ Can I see?

_____ Can I talk?

_____ Can I walk?

_____ Can I see, talk and walk at the same time?

_____ Did I drive home?

_____ Did I ride home?

_____ Am I home?

_____ If I rode home, who did I ride with?

_____ Did I ride and drive at the same time?

_____ Am I in the garage?

_____ Am I in *my* garage?

_____ Am I in a room other than the garage?

_____ Am I sick?

_____ Was I sick?

_____ Am I going to be sick?

_____ Did I throw up in the defroster again?

_____ Do I know my name?

_____ Can I say my name?

_____ Am I attracting fruit flies?

_____ Is this my car?

_____ Did I have a hat?

_____ Where are the fenders on the right side?

_____ Was the garage door open when I drove in?

_____ Is that me in the mirror?

_____ Why am I driving a bus?

_____ Are the people on the bus drunk?

_____ Should I give the people on the bus a transfer?

_____ Should I wait five minutes before I go in?

LOOK YOURSELF OVER...

CHECK LIST #2: AM I DRESSED?

If you cannot answer three or more of the following questions, do not go into the house.

_____ Do I have clothes on?

_____ Are they my clothes?

_____ Is this my underwear?

_____ Did my underwear always say, "Tuesday"?

_____ Why am I wearing a bra?

_____ Does the bra match my "Tuesday" panties?

_____ Was I wearing a dress this morning?

_____ Did I have shoes on when I left the house?

_____ Did they have three-inch heels?

_____ Why do my clothes smell of Mexican food?

_____ Where are my pants?

_____ Why am I wearing a blouse with sweat shields?

_____ Why am I speaking Spanish?

_____ Where did I get the tassle on my fly?

LOOK YOURSELF OVER...

CHECK LIST #3: DO I LOOK FUNNY?

In other words, "Have I left myself open for questions?" Are there little telltale markings I have overlooked? If you cannot answer the following questions quickly, you should consider getting a motel room until your mind clears.

____ Why is there lipstick on my shoes?

____ Why is there blonde hair on my coat?

____ Why is there blonde, brown and red hair on my pants?

____ Why am I dressed in a wet suit?

____ Why do I have whip marks on my legs?

____ When did I get a tattoo?

____ Why is this goat in my car?

____ Do I know the goat?

____ Why is the goat smiling at me?

____ Why am I covered with peanut butter?

____ Did I stop off to see my wife's bridge partner?

____ Does she still make homemade peanut butter?

____ Did I promise to get the goat into show business?

____ Should I get a motel room until my mind clears?

____ Should I take the goat with me?

4. THE ENTRANCE

The Number One rule is: never use the door. Your mate is bound to hear you. She may also put the night latch on, forcing you to "knock." Instead, if you have previously cut a trapdoor in the living room floor, you can gain access through the crawl space under the house. Of course, you should look through the window before using the trapdoor to make sure your wife is not standing on it.

5. THE STRIP

Take off your clothes before going into the bedroom. Never try to sit on the bed and undress. You will jiggle your wife awake.

(You should also make sure it is not your birthday, since your friends may be hiding in the house waiting to jump out and yell, "Surprise!")

6. THE TURN OFFS

Whatever is *on,* leave *on.* TV, radio, lights, water, heat, whatever...leave it *on.* The moment you turn anything off, she'll be wide awake and ready to start the interrogation.

7. THE TOILET

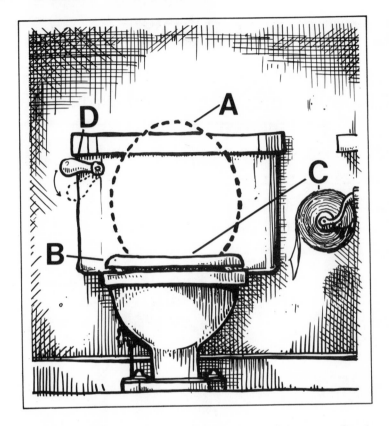

The best idea is not to use it. If you feel you must, keep these suggestions in mind:

(A) Don't bang the seat up.

(B) Sit down.

(C) Throw plenty of toilet paper in the toilet to muffle the sound.

(D) Do not flush.

8. THE BEDROOM

Getting into bed is the most important phase of the operation. You must begin by checking the bed for traps. Make sure you don't sit on one of the kids' "toot-and-go" toys. Make sure you don't sit on the cat.

Now sit on the bed slowly. Make sure

A — TOOT AND GO TOY

B — POTENTIAL HAZARD

C — EXTREME CAUTION

D — DO NOT USE

E — OBJECTIVE

Z — WHAT YOU DON'T WANT TO INTERRUPT·

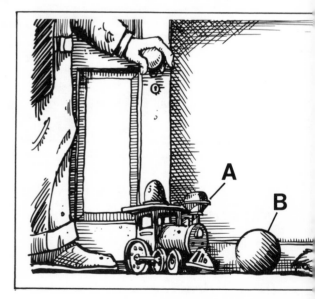

you still have your clothes with you. Slowly lie down. Once you are on the pillow, set your clothes down at this point. *If your wife wakes up, you jump up, grab your clothes and say you are getting dressed to go to work early.*

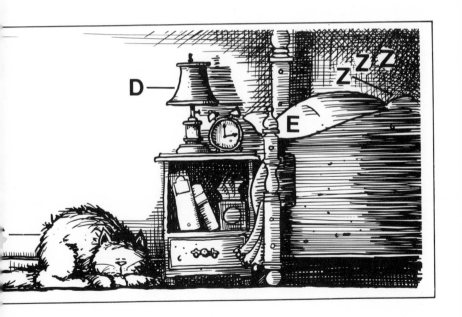

FOURTEEN SURE-FIRE EXCUSES TO EXPLAIN WHY YOU ARE LATE*

*Anywhere from five minutes to one year.

Being late has always been a big problem. To convincingly explain *why* you are late is an even bigger problem.

The key is: *get the story straight.* Cover all the angles. Much the way a cat operates in a fresh box of kitty litter. Locate the problem, then cover it.

How late you get home will determine how complex the excuse must be. But it has been scientifically proven that a little gift helps to fortify the excuse. On the following pages we have listed various excuses, appropriate gifts and estimated costs.

10 MINUTES LATE

EXCUSE

"Hi! I'm sorry I'm 10 minutes late."

GIFT SUGGESTION

None.

ESTIMATED COST

None.

≈ 20 MINUTES LATE ≈

EXCUSE

"Hi, Honey! Sorry I'm 20 minutes late."

GIFT SUGGESTION

None.

ESTIMATED COST

None.

NOTE: Be sure to punch-up *"Honey."*

≈ 30 MINUTES LATE ≈

EXCUSE

"Hi, Honey! I'm sorry I'm 30 minutes late. I've been walking around the house. We sure could use some new plants."

GIFT SUGGESTION

Plants.

ESTIMATED COST

None. (Just suggest the plants. Buying them is not necessary.)

~ 45 MINUTES LATE ~

EXCUSE

"Hi, Honey. I'm sorry I'm 45 minutes late. I stopped by Judy's Garden Supply. I asked her what would be nice this time of year and she said, "Why don't you try some of my Hollyhocks?" So I did."

GIFT SUGGESTION

Hollyhocks.

ESTIMATED COST

$6.65.

NOTE: Make sure it is not winter. If it is, grab a couple of pine cones.

1 HOUR LATE

EXCUSE

"Hi, Honey. I'm sorry I'm an hour late. I stopped by Judy's Garden Supply. I told her I was looking for something to stick in among the bushes for a little variety. She took me down to the greenhouse and gave me a few planting tips. She sure knows her stuff. By the way, I bought you this Magnolia tree."

GIFT SUGGESTION

Magnolia tree.

ESTIMATED COST

$46.

2 HOURS LATE

EXCUSE

"Hi, Honey. I'm sorry I'm a couple of hours late. My new secretary, Fifi, couldn't get her car started so I had to help her. I pushed her over to Bob's Garage and Motel to get her battery charged. And guess what? I won a free lube job. While I was there I bought you this complete set of Presidents' coins."

GIFT SUGGESTION

Presidents' coins.

ESTIMATED COST

$28 for the coins, plus $40 for Bob's housekeeper at the motel.

3 HOURS LATE

EXCUSE

"Hi, Honey. I'm sorry I'm three hours late. Charley couldn't bowl tonight so he sent his wife instead. I never saw anyone take so long to warm up. By the way, while I was there, I signed you up for the mixed doubles league. I thought you could be Charley's partner on Wednesday nights and I could bowl with Pinky on Friday."

GIFT SUGGESTION

Entrance fee for mixed doubles and a complete new lady's bowling outfit.

ESTIMATED COST

$72.

≈ 4 HOURS LATE ≈

EXCUSE

"Hi, Honey. I'm sorry I'm four hours late. I just stopped off to get my car washed and darned if Sally didn't talk me into getting a special super wax job. By the way, I bought you that new watch you wanted."

GIFT SUGGESTION

New watch.

ESTIMATED COST

$100 ($25 for the Timex and $75 for Boom-Boom Sally, the hot waxer at the Wash-a-drome).

NOTE: This excuse should not be used on a day when it's raining.

9 HOURS LATE

EXCUSE

"Hi, Honey. I'm sorry I'm late. I ran into these three female muggers. Two of them held me down while the other one took my wallet and poured liquor down my throat. I was thinking, maybe you should have your own checking account."

GIFT SUGGESTION

New checking account.

ESTIMATED COST

$250 first deposit.

～ *1 DAY LATE* ～

EXCUSE

"Hi, Honey. Sorry I'm late. I was driving home yesterday when I saw this semi-truck hauling a tank with a whale in it. I noticed there was a leak in the tank so I pulled the driver over. He told me to borrow a garden hose and to keep pouring water into the tank while he went to look for a salt shaker. I stayed with that whale till I was sure she was breathing easy. By the way, I bought you this new outfit. How do you like it?

GIFT SUGGESTION

Woman's outfit, including purse and fur piece.

ESTIMATED COST

$500.

NOTE: It helps to rub a dead fish on yourself.

1 WEEK LATE

EXCUSE

"Hi, Honey. Sorry I'm late. I went to the lodge meeting and the entertainment was two Indian maidens doing their native dances. They didn't have a ride home so I drove them to Phoenix in the camper. By the way, while I was there, I bought you a silver mine."

GIFT SUGGESTION

Forty acres of desert property.

ESTIMATED COST

Approximately $150.00 an acre. Plus $9.95 for a shovel.

≈ 1 MONTH LATE ≈

EXCUSE

"Hi, Honey. Sorry I'm late. This transvestite held me up and then forced me to go back to his apartment. I waited till he fell asleep, then I made a break for it. I was thinking, if things like this continue to happen, I could be away a lot. Maybe you should have your own business."

GIFT SUGGESTION

McDonald's franchise.

ESTIMATED COST

$40,000.

∽ *6 MONTHS LATE* ∽

EXCUSE

"Hi, Honey. I'm sorry I'm late. I went to a wake for my friend, Dale. His wife, Jugs, was really taking it badly. She was so sad, I decided to stay with her until she got ahold of herself. I would have called you but I didn't want to leave her bedside. By the way, I was thinking of sending you to the next Winter Olympics and buying you a little chalet."

GIFT SUGGESTION

Round trip ticket to the Olympics and one small chalet near the 70-meter ski jump.

ESTIMATED COST

$120,000 to $130,000 depending on the country.

∽ *1 YEAR LATE* ∽

EXCUSE

"Hi, Honey, I'm home. I hope you didn't pay the ransom. By the way, I was thinking of buying you Ohio."

GIFT SUGGESTION

Ohio.

ESTIMATED COST

Out of average person's range. You should consider divorce.

!

THE COUGH
FOR LIFE
OR
QUICK ANSWERS
FOR
"WHERE THE
HELL HAVE YOU
BEEN?"

If your partner should awaken and ask, "Where the hell have you been?" you must remember to cough before you begin to answer. During the time you cough, you must construct your entire answer, and it better be good. Your safety depends on that cough!

The questions on the following pages will illustrate the type of problems you could be faced with. Read the question, cough once, and answer quickly. Compare your answer to those that have been proven foolproof.

QUICK ANSWERS

QUESTION

"A Linda called and said to tell you that her brothers know everything. They are looking for you and are liable to bust your balls. What's that about?"

(COUGH!)

YOUR ANSWER

_____

_____

_____

_____

_____

_____

_____

_____

∾ *OUR ANSWER* ∾

"Oh, that's Linda down at the club. They upped the Christmas donation this year and I forgot. If you don't pay the donation the brothers take your charity Christmas ball decoration off the tree. I was going to buy two this year. It's for a good cause. Maybe I better run over to the club and straighten this out."

QUESTION

"A nurse called and said the tests are positive. She said you are supposed to take the penicillin pills for two weeks and then come in for a checkup."

(COUGH!)

YOUR ANSWER

_____

_____

_____

_____

_____

_____

_____

_____

∽ *OUR ANSWER* ∽

"Oh, great. Then it *is* my liver. They found it on the first test I guess. Remember when I ate that lobster the other night and had cramps. I guess it contained iodine. Say, you had the lobster too, didn't you? It might not be a bad idea for you to take the pills too. I'll run down to the drugstore and pick up a gross."

QUESTION

"Your picture's on the front page of today's paper. It says they raided a massage parlor and an officer is holding your arm. What is that all about?"

(COUGH!)

YOUR ANSWER

_____

_____

_____

_____

_____

_____

_____

_____

∾ *OUR ANSWER* ∾

"I had just given blood in the mobile unit parked next to the massage parlor when the raid took place. I went over to see what was going on. I didn't realize how weak I was. It's lucky that cop was there to catch me before I fainted. Pass the cream, will you Honey?"

DON'T FORGET YOUR FACE

Your face has a way of giving you away. Learn to know your face. There will be times when you'll be asked direct questions about your outside activities and you must be prepared to answer them without your face giving you away. This only comes through practice. Look directly into a mirror and practice the following replies without shifting your eyes or letting your mouth quiver.

Affect the following looks of innocence:

Once you have established a hurt, bewildered or deeply religious look you can respond to any inquisition with the following 10 successfully tested answers:

1. What?
2. Who told you that?
3. I've never been in the place.
4. It's probably red paint.
5. I was working.
6. Oh, come on.
7. I think I left my pants at the office, so what's the problem?
8. I stopped wearing underwear, why?
9. I don't even know her.
10. I always eat lunch at the massage parlor. They have a great little coffee shop.

TEN FOOLPROOF ANSWERS FOR HICKIES, LIPSTICK SMEARS AND SCRATCHES ON THE BACK

TRANSFERRING THE GUILT

These answers are designed to make her carry the guilt. Remember—when she apologizes, be gracious.

1. I'm going out because I got a call from an old buddy who is about to kill himself if he doesn't have someone to confide in and you ask me, "Where are you going at three o'clock in the morning?"

2. A dying mother who hasn't seen her son in almost 11 years because of some stupid family argument gives me a personal article of hers to give to him to show she still cares about him, and you ask me, "What's a brassiere doing in my glove compartment?"

3. A cosmetic salesman was fast-thinking enough to throw his sample case in front of me to keep me from getting hit by a cab and you ask me, "How about that lipstick on your pants?"

4. I happen to spot a kid being attacked by an octopus and after struggling with the most dangerous of all creatures of the sea, you ask me, "Who has been sucking on your neck?"

5. I ride a horse six miles through the underbrush to pick you fresh raspberries and you ask me, "Who has been clawing at your back?"

6. I apprehend a crazy midget trying to attack a woman in an elevator and you ask me, "Who bit you in the ass?"

7. I cured your cold with chicken soup, I cured your backache with a massage, I cured your sprained wrist with an ace bandage, and now you question me when I want you to take three lousy penicillin shots?

8. What the hell is wrong with you? How often do I ask you to shave off every hair on your body?

9.   Don't you understand — Dave can't
     go on the sales convention trip to
     the Virgin Islands because he's the
     president of the company and he
     can't be out of touch with the
     business that long. Now do you
     understand why I'm taking two
     secretaries?

10. I do a magic show for those poor
     kids in the children's ward and I see
     those little faces brighten up and
     those smiles go from ear to ear, and
     you sit there and ask me why I
     want to buy a condo for the head
     nurse?

TEN THINGS
NOT TO DO

THINGS NOT TO DO

You should avoid the following situations. They are trouble-makers and can lead to questions you may not be able to answer.

1. Never take Sodium Pentothal. Even for major surgery.

2. Do not take a female friend to televised sports events.

3. If you keep a diary, make sure you can eat it.

4. Do not bolt up in your own bed and say, "I've got to get home."

5. Do not talk about the latest adult movies.

6. Do not try to fill a waterbed with a high pressure fire hose.

7. Never let anyone scratch your back with a ballpoint pen.

8. Never call home while breathing hard.

9. Never bring your gorgeous friend from the office over to the house for Christmas and introduce her as an orphan.

10. Do not call your house and ask if you're home yet.

THE
OTHER
WOMAN

If circumstances have been unfortunate enough to force you into "supplementing" your marriage with another woman, you may find that this woman will also have questions from time to time. One question you might hear is the ever popular, "WHEN THE HELL ARE YOU GETTING A DIVORCE?"

As a famous juggler once said, "Putting the balls in the air is not the problem—keeping them there is." The following suggestions are made to help you keep your balls in the air. There are several popular locations where the dreaded question, "When the hell are you getting a divorce?" may arise. The following locations and suitable juggling devices may be used in response to the question.

THE OTHER WOMAN....

IN A RESTAURANT

When you are out with the other woman in a restaurant and she asks about a divorce, it can be a testy situation unless you are prepared. Always carry a plastic bag full of fish, chicken and steak bones. Upon hearing the question, pop the appropriate bone in your mouth and give the international sign for choking. Continue to choke until you feel the question is only a memory. If you are a vegetarian, you should also carry a potato bug or a garden trowel that you can easily pop in your mouth when the question is broached.

IN THE THEATER

If she confronts you with the question while watching a movie or play, immediately turn around and smack the person directly behind you. There is usually a physical response on the other person's part. Ask the person to step outside and settle the matter. Do not reenter the theater until you are certain the question is no longer of primary importance.

AT A SPORTING EVENT

Stand up in the stadium or arena and shout something about the hometown team. For instance, if you are watching a Cowboys football game, try yelling, *"Dallas Sucks!"* Do not expect to see your friend for at least a week, since stitches will probably be required.

AT THE BEACH

If the question is asked while you are in the water, go at once to the bottom of the pool or ocean and walk as far as you can. If you are not in the water, set your bathing suit on fire, run to the water, and walk on the bottom as far as you can. If you see others walking on the bottom, do not stop to chat; you will need the air.

IN THE MOTEL ROOM

Always bring a trained dog with you.
The dog should be trained to bite you in
the groin when he hears the phrase,
"How about the divorce?" He should be
trained to hold on until you see fit to
give the command, "Let go of them, boy."
You should also caution the girl not to
try and hit the dog in the head with a 2x4.
Oft times she is not accurate and the blow
is worse than the bite.

WHILE DRIVING

This is the easiest of all situations to overcome. Always carry a stuffed (or dead) dog in the trunk of your car. When she mentions the divorce, turn the wheel sharply and shout, *"Oh, my God!"* Stop the car, take the dog out of the trunk and throw it under the car. If this effect is used fairly often, the color of the dog should be changed from time to time.

Pre-planned distractions are often the best and quickest way to avoid answering the dreaded **"WHEN ARE YOU GETTING A DIVORCE?"** question. The 10 most popular distractions, not necessarily in order of preference, are listed below. They can be used any time and any place. They could save your life and your marriage.

1. Be able to throw up at a moment's notice. This is often done by drinking a glass of milk with a spoonful of lard in it.
2. Practice falling out of a hotel window. Start with the second floor and work your way up.
3. Learn to break any major bone in your body.
4. Practice slipping into a coma.
5. Try to overcome the fear of shooting yourself.
6. Learn to annoy a cop.
7. Do not be afraid to wet your pants.
8. Do not be afraid to wet somebody else's pants.
9. Run over yourself with the car.
10. Above all, do not show shock when you hear the question. This can be accomplished by wearing a stocking over your face at all times.

ABOUT THE AUTHOR

He's famous.